# Seven Answers

## — *for* —

## Anxiety

**GREGORY L. JANTZ, PHD**
**WITH ANN MCMURRAY**

AspirePress

Carson, California

AspirePress

Seven Answers for Anxiety
Copyright © 2016 Gregory L. Jantz
All rights reserved.
Aspire Press, an imprint of Rose Publishing, Inc.
17909 Adria Maru Lane
Carson, CA 90746 USA
www.aspirepress.com

Register your book at www.aspirepress.com/register
and receive a FREE *How to Study the Bible* PDF
to print for your personal or ministry use.

Printed in the United States of America
020217LSC

# Contents

# *The* Chicken Little Life

*Patty* was a worrier, ever since she could remember. As a child, she was acutely aware of anything in her world that could go wrong. Things that went wrong usually meant pain of some kind. Only by being alert and watchful for those wrong things could Patty attempt to keep herself safe—or, at least, safer. As a child, Patty rarely felt safe.

Patty grew up into a serious, cautious adult. Risks were to be avoided. Control over her circumstances was essential. Patty was meticulous and highly organized, not out of a desire for positive results but out of a fear of negative consequences. Safety could only occur when people and circumstances could be planned for and controlled. As an adult, Patty rarely felt safe.

Patty grew to resent and envy others who could live life so relaxed and unconcerned, including members of her own family. Someone had to be the responsible one and Patty resigned herself to that position. When decisions were to be made, Patty was always the one to point out the problems. Murphy's Law—anything that can go wrong will go wrong—was not a joke for Patty. Murphy's Law was how Patty lived her life and she resigned herself to repeatedly saying, "I told you so." Whenever something did go wrong, Patty began to feel vindicated and, in a strange way, relieved.

## A Bundle of Nerves

The older Patty got, however, the harder control became and the more she had to worry about. She worried about her family, her kids in particular. She worried about her job and her husband's job; she worried about how they were going to pay the bills today and still have anything left for tomorrow. She worried about where they lived and what was happening in the schools and on the streets. She worried about her health and the health of her family. The more she digested the news, the sicker she became over the problems and dangers and wrong things in the world. The less control she felt, the more desperate and negative she became with everyone. People who knew Patty called her a bundle of nerves.

Her family could be less charitable. Patty's attempt to keep her kids from danger was interpreted by them—often loudly and angrily—as interference. Patty's recitations of the cons in any decision resulted in her husband isolating her from more and more of those decisions.

All Patty wanted was to keep everyone safe, but they treated her like she was the danger. All she wanted was to keep everyone safe, but instead she was still being punished. There was no gratitude, no appreciation for all she did for them. As time went on, Patty felt herself increasingly isolated from family and friends who refused to admit she was right to worry and had a right to worry.

> JESUS SAID, "COME TO ME, ALL YOU WHO ARE WEARY AND BURDENED, AND I WILL GIVE YOU REST."
> —MATTHEW 11:28

## The Burden of Worry

Patty was used to shouldering the burden of worry. The weight had been familiar and almost comfortable—but not anymore. Now, even getting out of bed was almost insurmountable. Her only motivation to engage in the day was the fear of losing her job and losing track of her teens. She worried that she wasn't doing well at either of those jobs. Several times, she'd been sure she was having some sort of seizure, insisting she be taken to the emergency room where she'd been diagnosed with panic attacks. Now the person she'd always relied upon to manage in the midst of her anxieties—herself—was compromised.

On edge about her health and feeling detached and misunderstood by others, Patty felt imprisoned by worries spiraling out of control. Nothing seemed to be working. Everything that could go wrong was, and Patty had no idea what to do.

■ ■ ■

Does Patty's story sound similar to yours? If so, welcome to the Chicken Little Life.

I grew up hearing the story of Chicken Little, never dreaming I would find it so applicable in my professional work with adults. For children, the story of Chicken Little is about what happens to a group of cute-sounding animals. For adults, the story of Chicken Little is a cautionary tale about three dangers: thought-life, hidden assumptions, and mistaken beliefs.

"Chicken Little" is the title of the story, but that title doesn't really convey its full scope. If it were up to me, I'd subtitle the story of Chicken Little: *From an Acorn to the End of the World.*

For those of you who can't remember or never heard this charming children's tale, here it is in a nutshell (pun intended): Chicken Little one day goes into the forest where an acorn falls on her head. She cries out, "The sky is falling! The sky is falling!" and runs off to tell the king. Along the way, she meets up with Henny Penny, Goosey Loosey, and Ducky Lucky, who join her in a panicked rush to inform the king of impending disaster.

This group of fowl runs into Foxy Loxy, who offers his help to tell the king. What Foxy Loxy, being a fox, actually does is lure the frantic chicken, hen, goose, and duck into his den where he gobbles them up.

## Danger #1: Thought-Life

The danger to Chicken Little, it turns out, wasn't what she had thought it was. She had thought she was in danger from an impending celestial apocalypse of the sky falling. That wasn't the danger. The danger wasn't even the acorn, though I'm sure it hurt when it hit. The danger to Chicken Little was her own anxiety-driven conclusion about the acorn. Chicken Little was so concerned about the false danger from acorns, she forgot about the real danger from foxes.

### Internal v. External Danger

At the beginning of the story, the danger to Chicken Little was an internal one—her mind. At the end of the story, the danger to Chicken Little was an external one—the fox. This is the essence of anxiety-driven fear—the internal overshadows the external; thoughts of *what if* overshadow the reality of *what is*. By concentrating on the imaginary danger, Chicken Little failed to recognize the real one.

People do the same thing in real life on a regular basis. Have you ever found yourself noticing something small that starts to get bigger and bigger the more anxious you become? Say there's a mole on the back of your leg. It's always been there, but you haven't really paid attention to it. All of a sudden, you notice the mole and become anxious. Why have you just noticed it? Has it changed color? Something could be wrong! Moles that change color mean cancer. In your mind, anxiety has taken you from a mole you've never thought about to a mole with cancer.

**ANXIETY IS PRODUCED BY WHAT YOU TELL YOURSELF.**

Chicken Little could have said, "Ouch! I got hit with an acorn," and determined to avoid walking under trees. Instead, she insisted, "The sky is falling!" Acorns fall all the time, but the sky does not. One is common; the other is cataclysmic.

## What is Anxiety?

Anxiety is defined as "painful or apprehensive uneasiness of the mind usually over an impending or anticipated ill; fearful concern or interest; ... an abnormal or overwhelming sense of apprehension and fear often marked by physiological signs (as sweating, tension, and increased pulse), by doubt concerning the reality and nature of the threat, and by self-doubt about one's capacity to cope with it."

When anxiety takes over, you are propelled out of the realm of the probable and into the improbable. Anxiety accelerates the common into the cataclysmic at rapid speed. Anxiety, then, is produced not by what you actually experience but by what you tell yourself; your thoughts determine your reality. When those thoughts are anxious, anxiety is what you'll experience, no matter what is really happening. What you tell yourself—your thought-life—matters.

Everyone has a thought-life, the inner dialogue that goes on in your head. Some people barely recognize those thoughts are there, running in the background of their lives. Others experience their thought-life as a semi-audible conversation, inhabited with the voices and messages of people from their past and present.

Anxious people spend a great deal of time in a what-if world. Once anxiety is triggered, a person can go from zero (calm) to sixty (panicked) in seconds, generally through a series of rapid-fire inner questions with correspondingly dire answers.

**What could happen?** → **The worst**

**What does it mean?** → **Disaster**

**What will happen to me?** → **Something horrible**

In the rush to anxious judgment, there's rarely time to investigate those questions. Are they even valid? Where do those questions come from? When your thought-life naturally defaults to disaster, you will naturally experience disaster.

One of the ways to combat such a thought-life is to intentionally push out the negative with the positive.

"Whatever is true, whatever is noble, whatever is right, whatever is pure, whatever is lovely, whatever is admirable—if anything is excellent or praiseworthy— think about such things" (Philippians 4:8). When you turn your thought-life toward God—who is all these things—you take the focus off of you and your disasters.

## Danger #2: Hidden Assumptions

In my experience, behind each panicked question lies a hidden assumption. Chicken Little assumed the sky was falling. Why? Clearly that hadn't happened in the past or Chicken Little would have no present. What was it about her thought-life that allowed such an assumption?

Chicken Little must have assumed that disaster was just a bonk-in-the-head away from happening. Behind the panic of anxiety is a storehouse of hidden assumptions. Uncovering this trove of assumptions, then, becomes vital to understanding the basis for anxiety.

People with anxiety spend so much time dealing with the present consequences of their anxiety, they seldom have the time or energy to go back to the root causes— those hidden assumptions. Because these assumptions remain hidden, they take on the mantle of fact. But an assumption is not necessarily a fact.

You may assume the reason you've noticed a mole is because it's changed color and is now cancerous. However, how did you know the mole changed color if you hadn't noticed it before? You assumed you noticed it now because it had changed color due to cancer, but that is only an assumption. An assumption is something taken for granted. Things taken for granted tend to bypass serious inspection.

The hidden assumptions behind anxiety are no different. They become part of a personal lexicon of absolutes. With anxiety, however, these absolutes are negative and create a pervasive climate of negativity. People are different, with different hidden assumptions undergirding their thought-life but, for anxious people, I've found a common thread:

> One of the ways to combat such a thought-life is to intentionally push out the negative with the positive.
>
> "WHATEVER IS TRUE, WHATEVER IS NOBLE, WHATEVER IS RIGHT, WHATEVER IS PURE, WHATEVER IS LOVELY, WHATEVER IS ADMIRABLE —IF ANYTHING IS EXCELLENT OR PRAISEWORTHY— THINK ABOUT SUCH THINGS" — PHILIPPIANS 4:8

## UNWORTHINESS

*"I deserve to have bad things happen to me."*

One of the most damaging hidden assumptions you can make is that you're not worthy of good things happening to you. When bad things happen, you accept this as the way the world is supposed to work. If something good happens, you become anxious, convinced something bad has to happen to return the world to its balanced, negative order.

## LACK OF ABILITY

*"I do not have the skills or ability to overcome this problem."*

If you assume you're not able to handle whatever life throws your way, you probably won't. Each new failure props up this assumption. And each new day brings another opportunity for you, and the rest of the world, to receive proof positive that you're incapable and incompetent. Each new task, then, carries its own seed for disaster.

## ■ INADEQUACY

*"I am not good enough or strong enough to overcome this problem."*

The assumption of inadequacy is different from lack of ability. The fear of your inability is a fear of what you do; anxiety over inadequacy is a fear of who you are. This fear says you are not enough; you are insufficient as a person and no matter what you do, however good it might be, will ever make up for your fundamental inadequacy as a person.

> Whenever you feel inadequate or unworthy, remember who it is that created you.
>
> "FOR WE ARE GOD'S HANDIWORK, CREATED IN CHRIST JESUS TO DO GOOD WORKS, WHICH GOD PREPARED IN ADVANCE FOR US TO DO."
> —EPHESIANS 2:10

## ■ ABANDONMENT

*"Because I'm a failure, others will reject me."*

If you assume you're not worthy or are incapable or inadequate, then you assume people don't really want to be with you. You assume people will leave. The future becomes a minefield for pain, confusion, and fear where you alone are left to suffer the inevitable negative consequences of being unworthy, unable, and inadequate.

Hidden assumptions undermine your sense of self. They weaken your concept of who you are, through the constant negative messages of your thought-life. Assumptions, however, have one small advantage: if caught in time, assumptions can sometimes be changed by an examination of outside factors.

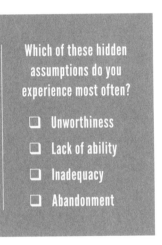

**Which of these hidden assumptions do you experience most often?**

❏ Unworthiness
❏ Lack of ability
❏ Inadequacy
❏ Abandonment

Changing assumptions can prove difficult, but when an assumption becomes a belief, change becomes even more challenging. In order to overcome anxiety, it's important, then, to keep hidden assumptions from solidifying into mistaken beliefs.

# Danger #3: Mistaken Beliefs

Mistaken beliefs are those things you are convinced are true, even when faced with solid evidence to the contrary. Assumptions may be released, but beliefs can be clung to with dogged determination. Often, these mistaken beliefs are created in childhood and used in adulthood to cope with the stresses and strains of anxiety. In other words, what starts as survival mechanisms in childhood ends up becoming entrenched faulty belief systems in adulthood.

## ■ PERSONALIZATION

*"I am responsible for everything that happens to me."*

When you believe you are somehow responsible for everything that happens around you, you live in the eye of the storm. In this mistaken belief, there are no chances or accidents. Life becomes exceptionally personal—anything that goes wrong is all about you. Life is out to get you; people are out to get you; events are out to get you.

Therefore, you must constantly be on your guard. Like Patty, you live out Murphy's Law—anything bad that can happen to you will happen to you because you are you; therefore, you are never safe.

## ■ CONTROL

*"Life will fall apart if I'm not on top of everything and everyone."*

When you believe you are a cosmic target for bad things, you may decide your only protection is to try to control events and other people. This mistaken belief asserts that control brings safety.

*"I need someone else to make life safe for me."*

Some people personalize the negative, dealing with their anxiety by drawing it in to themselves in order to control it. Other people, though, deal with their anxiety by abdicating control, maneuvering themselves into the orbit and influence of others. This mistaken belief says that because there is no safety in self, then safety must be found in others.

## ■ PERFECTIONISM

*"I am a failure unless I meet my own high standards."*

If control brings safety, then control is mandatory. Events and people, though, are notoriously hard to control. When these slippery things that can cause you anxiety aren't controllable—but you must have control—then you mistakenly believe that safety is found by controlling yourself. You may believe that the closer you are to perfection, the farther you'll be from danger.

Sounds good, in a way, but there are two major problems with this belief:

1. Perfect is an impossible standard. Where perfect becomes the standard for safety, anything less is disaster.

2. If no one is perfect, than your own definition of perfect is, by definition, imperfect. Not only is perfect impossible to achieve, but your idea of perfect may also not actually produce the results you want.

All of these mistaken beliefs are ways to manage anxiety; they are not methods to remove anxiety. Instead of decreasing and de-escalating anxiety, these mistaken beliefs often serve to preserve anxiety. Using mistaken beliefs to manage anxiety is just another way of ensuring anxiety's continued presence in your life.

**LIVING WITH RUNAWAY FEAR AND CONSTANT ANXIETY ARE NOT HEALTHY WAYS TO LIVE.**

Anxious people desperately try to manage their anxiety, because they view anxiety itself as negative. But is anxiety always a negative? There are legitimate things in this world that should warrant your concern, so being anxious—in and of itself—can be a natural reaction:

- Being anxious is natural if a loved one is engaged in something inherently dangerous, such as military service.

- Being anxious is natural if you anticipate a major change in your life, such as marriage or the birth of a child.

- Being anxious is natural if you're stretched in some way, such as giving a major presentation at work.

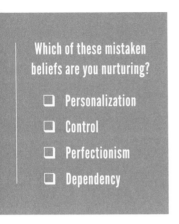

**Which of these mistaken beliefs are you nurturing?**

- ❏ Personalization
- ❏ Control
- ❏ Perfectionism
- ❏ Dependency

However, living with runaway fear and constant anxiety are not healthy ways to live. Like Chicken Little, anxiety can cause you to run blindly toward the true dangers in your world.

No one is able to remove all anxiety from life, because feeling anxious and fearful is a part of human nature. Anxiety isn't, in itself, wrong. A little anxiety is normal, but too much is damaging. So what is too little and how much is too much? Those are the questions of anxiety. Now let's look at the answers.

# Stop Feeding *the* Monster

*Glad* to be home, Carrie dropped her purse just inside the front door and sloughed off her shoes. The week had been rough, and she was looking forward to some peace and quiet. The guys were off hiking for the weekend, and as she worked her way into the kitchen, Carrie realized the house was a little too quiet. There were plenty of dirty dishes in the sink but no note good-bye.

She wondered what time they'd been able to get away. Driving home, she'd heard about a big wreck on the freeway. The thought flitted across her mind that, depending upon when the guys got away, they could have been on that stretch of road when the accident occurred.

Carrie tried to put it out of her mind, but the thought stayed stuck through dinner. About to watch a movie,

Carrie just couldn't settle down. The worry nagged at her. Finally, she gave in and called first her husband's phone and then her son's. Neither picked up.

That could mean anything, but why would both of them not answer? Could something have happened? Were they okay? She'd been looking forward to peace and quiet; now those were the farthest things from her mind.

All through the evening, Carrie was completely beside herself with worry. Then her husband finally called. He barely got two words in before she started yelling at him over the phone.

When she finally calmed down long enough to listen, she learned that, yes, they'd taken the interstate and, yes, they'd come up on the accident, so they'd gotten off and gone to a movie until the traffic cleared, which was why both of their phones were off. The only disaster was to Carrie's peace-and-quiet evening, because she had spent the evening feeding the anxiety monster for nothing.

■ ■ ■

# Starve *the* Anxiety Monster

Anxiety becomes the monster in the room that never goes away. And why should the monster go away when your thought-life—your hidden assumptions and your mistaken beliefs—keep feeding it? Every worried question, every anxious conclusion, every panicked response feeds the monster. The bigger the monster becomes, the more tyrannized you feel by the monster. Your life seems locked in a battle between you and the monster of anxiety.

**LOOKING AT LIFE OBJECTIVELY STARVES THE MONSTER. LOOKING AT LIFE SUBJECTIVELY FEEDS THE MONSTER.**

## Objectivity v. Subjectivity

How you look at life matters. There is a huge difference between looking at life objectively and looking at life subjectively. Looking at life objectively can starve the monster, while looking at life subjectively can feed the monster.

Merriam-Webster's dictionary says objectivity is found "in the realm of sensible experience independent of individual thought and perceptible by all observers: having reality independent of the mind." Objectivity recognizes that the mind can sometimes really mess you up, so you search for the truth of something beyond just what you think about it.

On the other hand, subjectivity is "characteristic of or belonging to reality as perceived rather than as independent of mind." Living your life mired in a subjective perspective means being trapped within what you perceive. If your perception is tethered to a thought-life full of hidden assumptions and mistaken beliefs, you can find yourself stuck in that negativity, constantly feeding the monster.

**THERE IS MORE TO REALITY THAN HOW YOU FEEL.**

Objectivity is a challenging concept for many anxious people. They find it difficult to admit the possibility that what happens is a reality that doesn't depend upon how they feel. Their truth is the only truth because of how deeply they feel that truth. *Whatever I feel must be the truth.*

Whatever you feel is certainly the truth of what you feel, but there is more to reality than how you feel.

Finding those other perspectives is the essence of being objective.

Consider Carrie's story. Halfway into a movie that she barely paid attention to, she was convinced her husband and son were lying injured on the interstate. Her perceived reality took their projected travel route, the freeway pile-up, the unanswered cell phone calls, and her own surety of disaster and created a disaster in her mind.

> You will find help when you reach out and explain the situation to wise people, avoiding Chicken Little followers.
>
> "PLANS FAIL FOR LACK OF COUNSEL, BUT WITH MANY ADVISERS THEY SUCCEED."
> —PROVERBS 15:22

Carrie subjectively thought of disaster, but what did she objectively know? She knew her husband and son left the house, but she didn't really know when. She knew there was a pile-up on the freeway, but she really didn't know what route the guys had taken. She knew they didn't answer their cell phones, but she really didn't know why.

# OBJECTIVITY V. SUBJECTIVITY

## Objectivity

- Objectivity is determining not only what you do know but also what you don't know.

- Objectivity is looking outside of yourself to help you evaluate the truth of a given situation.

- Objectivity asks questions like, "What are the odds?"

## Subjectivity

- Subjectivity causes an anxious person to reach a definite conclusion based upon very little evidence.

- Subjectivity concludes while objectivity evaluates.

- Subjectivity needs no further evidence than its own perception.

Move objective knowledge away from subjective perceptions. An excellent place to start is by asking:

- What are the odds?
- What are the facts?

Facts are what can be seen and agreed to by others outside of self. If you have trouble seeing beyond your own perceptions, ask for help from people you trust.

## Turn *a* What-If *into an* If-What

Anxious people can become consumed with the helplessness they feel in a what-if world. In a what-if world, disasters wait around every corner. In a what-if world, the person feels like a piece of flotsam on a vast, turbulent ocean, tossed about by the winds of misfortune, drowning in a sea of misery. A person in a what-if world feels like a helpless victim of circumstance. But in any given circumstance, are you really helpless?

You may need to ask yourself, *If the thing I fear were to happen, what could I do?* This allows you to turn a what-if into an if-what.

A what-if worldview concentrates on what isn't possible. An if-what worldview concentrates on what is possible. Say, for example, you're anxious about losing your job. You look over the facts, such as your last several evaluations, and calculate the odds of being let go. Even though your reviews were good and the odds of being fired are small, the size of your fear about losing your job just keeps overshadowing your objectivity. But ask yourself, *If I did lose my job, what could I do?*

Anxiety says that losing your job is the sky falling. But does it have to be? Subjectively, you may want to say yes, but objectively the truth is no. There are plenty of examples of people who lost jobs and found new jobs, even jobs they liked better. People who have lost jobs have gone on to discover new interests, new careers. A job loss has led to uncovering new talents and new priorities. Suppose the following example on page 33 is about you.

Moving from subjective to objective means asking yourself some questions (*What are the odds? What are the facts? If what I fear were to happen, what could I do?*), instead of taking everything you're telling yourself for granted.

Practice moving from subjective responses to objective responses by writing your responses to these three questions:

- What is my current fear?

- What is the likelihood of it happening based on the facts?

- If this were to happen, what could I do?

---

| **MY CURRENT FEAR:**

*Losing my job*

| **WHAT IS THE LIKELIHOOD OF IT HAPPENING BASED ON THE FACTS?**

*All of my reviews have been good. Although there may have been minor improvements I needed to make, the reviews have been positive.*

| **IF THIS WERE TO HAPPEN, WHAT COULD I DO?**

*I would start by looking for a new job online and by asking others—my trusted friends, family, and neighbors. I might get some training for a different job. I might look a little further away. I would work on my interviewing skills.*

---

## MY CURRENT FEAR:


## WHAT IS THE LIKELIHOOD OF IT HAPPENING BASED ON THE FACTS?


## IF THIS WERE TO HAPPEN, WHAT COULD I DO?

| MY CURRENT FEAR:

| WHAT IS THE LIKELIHOOD OF IT HAPPENING BASED ON THE FACTS?

| IF THIS WERE TO HAPPEN, WHAT COULD I DO?

# Control *the* Volume

When you automatically give in to your negative thought-life—to your hidden assumptions and mistaken beliefs—you feed the monster. This, again, is why it's important for you to know what you're whispering to yourself. The only way to really hear those subtle messages that run in the background of your mind is to start paying more attention and turn up the volume.

> You can turn the volume way down by steering clear of negative people and situations and by asking the Lord to guard your mind.
>
> "DISCRETION WILL PROTECT YOU, AND UNDERSTANDING WILL GUARD YOU."
> —PROVERB 2:11

When you become anxious or fearful, instead of reacting to the fear, evaluate the fear. What are you telling yourself will happen? Why have you come to that conclusion? Where does the fear come from? Who told you life was supposed to turn out that way? Who told you that *you* were supposed to turn out that way?

Again, the negative, anxious messages that keep looping in your mind often come from your past. When you keep listening to and living in the past, you short-change today and tomorrow. The fear of the past drains away all the promise of the future. But in order to move beyond your past, you need to endure the pain of turning up the volume on those negative messages from your past, so you can really hear them and objectively evaluate them.

Negative messages need to be turned up, but only so you can evaluate them; they are not meant to be cranked up for the rest of your life. The goal of turning up the volume on negative thoughts is so you can really hear what they're saying and learn to put those messages in their proper context. These thoughts, after all, are a part of you, but you've given them far too much power and authority over you. Understanding who you are and how these messages have affected your life is important, which is how you put them into their proper context.

## ■ TURN DOWN THE VOLUME

Once you've become familiar with what these messages are and what and whom they come from, then you're ready to start intentionally turning the volume back down. Turning up the volume on these messages means taking control over them. Turning down the volume on these messages means taking control over them. Learn to control

the volume and you learn to control the messages
that feed the monster.

## REFUSE TO LISTEN TO NEGATIVE MESSAGES

As you work on controlling the volume of your
negative messages, you may find yourself saying
to those messages, "Yes, I hear you, but I choose
not to react to you." You may find yourself saying,
"Yes, I hear you, but I've decided to turn your
volume way down."

## ■ REPLACE NEGATIVE MESSAGES WITH POSITIVE MESSAGES

Realize, however, that turning down the volume on the negative may not be enough. You may need to say, "Yes, I hear you, but I'm choosing to listen to positive messages instead." It may not be enough to rid yourself of negative messages; you may need to fill that empty space with positive messages.

## ■ CHANGE THE CHANNEL

You may find that you need to treat your mind like you do the radio in your car: if you hear a song you don't like, change the channel!

But how do you find that different, positive channel? One of the best ways I know of is to practice being positive.

> **Positive messages from the Bible:**
>
> "I CAN DO ALL THIS THROUGH HIM WHO GIVES ME STRENGTH."
> —PHILIPPIANS 4:13
>
> "I PRAY THAT OUT OF HIS GLORIOUS RICHES HE MAY STRENGTHEN YOU WITH POWER THROUGH HIS SPIRIT IN YOUR INNER BEING."
> —EPHESIANS 3:16
>
> "STAND FIRM IN THE FAITH; BE COURAGEOUS; BE STRONG."
> —1 CORINTHIANS 16:13B

You need to practice being optimistic. A pessimist is someone who expects bad things to happen. An optimist is someone who expects good things to happen.

Anytime you begin to practice a new skill, it seems strange. Because the new skill doesn't come naturally, you need to concentrate on what you're doing. The Bible is full of God's love and his enduring promises. The Bible is the most positive book you'll ever read and it has the most positive, greatest story ever told. Where else are you going to read how the God of the universe loves you and set out a plan from the beginning of time to show you his love?

For too long, you've been listening to your own voice of fear coloring your world. That monster you've been feeding is loud and demanding. That monster has been growing and growing and taking up so much space

The Bible says the Lord loves you and cares for you:

"I AM WITH YOU ALWAYS, TO THE VERY END OF THE AGE."
—MATTHEW 28:20

"THE LORD IS CLOSE TO THE BROKENHEARTED AND SAVES THOSE WHO ARE CRUSHED IN SPIRIT."
—PSALM 34:18

"CAST ALL YOUR ANXIETY ON HIM BECAUSE HE CARES FOR YOU."
—1 PETER 5:7

in your world that you've had difficulty seeing anything positive at all. God is bigger than your fears and more powerful than your monster. God is the eternal optimist. He knows good things will happen, because he has promised those good things; and when God promises, he delivers.

**GOD IS BIGGER THAN YOUR FEARS AND MORE POWERFUL THAN YOUR MONSTER.**

It's time to switch to a different channel, a good channel, a God channel. Fill up your mind, heart, and soul with positive, uplifting messages. Surround yourself with positive messages that you can hear and see as constant reminders of God's love and care for you.

- Start and end each day with a devotional thought, a prayer of thanks.

- Watch for the good God brings into your world.

- Smell a flower.

- Kiss a child.

- Enjoy a sunset.

God's beauty and goodness can be found in the most unexpected places, even within yourself.

## Do This *for* 30 Days:

1. Write down three things you're thankful for today.

2. Write three to five sentences about one positive experience today.

3. Send a thank-you or a word of encouragement to someone in your family, a friend, a coworker, a past acquaintance, or someone who has experienced tragedy (maybe someone in the news).

If you do this for a month, you will notice that you'll start to naturally look for positive things all day.

# Right-Size *the* Small Stuff

**When** Mark's wife asked him to get the mail, he felt like throwing something.

Why would he want to get the mail? The mail was full of bills he had to pay.

Why would he want to get the mail? The mail was full of warnings about things he had to deal with, from product recalls to compromised credit cards.

Why would he want to get the mail? He had a pile of the stuff sitting on his desk that he didn't have energy to deal with now.

Why would he want to get the mail? Or answer his phone? Or check his email? Why would he subject himself to one more task, one more demand, one more must-do thing, when he couldn't seem to get anything done?

Why would he want to get the mail?

■ ■ ■

Getting the mail shouldn't seem like an insurmountable obstacle. Anxieties create a life on overload. When you worry about everything, that kind of pressure takes its toll. The accumulated weight of anxiety can make climbing molehills seem like scaling mountains. Over time, the accumulated weight of anxiety can make even small things, like getting the mail, too great a task. There is no such thing as small stuff. All stuff becomes big stuff.

The more anxious you feel, the less able you may be to determine what constitutes a true crisis. When there is no small stuff, all stuff must be treated as a potential crisis, fraught with risk and potential disaster—even something as mundane as getting the mail. High anxiety is a life lived among the klaxon bells of red alert.

## Accept *the* Small Stuff

### Taking It Personally . . . Or Not

One of the mistaken beliefs talked about earlier was personalization—that everything that happens centers around you. This mistaken belief can take on a life of its own when you are in anxiety overload. You become a raw nerve, jumping at everything that happens around you and at everyone you come into contact with. In such a state, there is no such thing as a misspoken word, a casual comment, a harmless mistake, a misunderstanding.

Personalizing everything that happens to you is a form of self-absorption. This level of self-absorption leads to a sense of martyrdom. Martyrdom alienates you from people and from the truth. Under this sense of siege— this state of martyrdom—nothing is neutral. When the world itself and the people in it always seem to be against you, the only person you listen to is yourself. When all you do is listen to yourself, you feed the monster.

## Taking Control ... Or Not

A vital answer to anxiety is learning to right-size the small stuff. First you need to stand down from siege mode and realize there actually is small stuff. Not everything that happens is about you.

- Sometimes, there's traffic on a road you want to travel.

- Sometimes, the line you're in will inexplicably move slower than the line next to you.

- Sometimes, a product sent to you will be miss-picked.

This is the randomness that happens in the utterly complex dance known as life. These events are not orchestrated to thwart your will or derail your plans or punish you in any way. In the game of life, dice are not rigged to come up snake eyes just for you.

Accepting the small stuff means allowing events and people to act without assuming they are acting because of you. In a similar way, accepting the small stuff means accepting, in large part, that events and people cannot be controlled, no matter how much you wish you could. Accepting the small stuff means accepting that the only thing you have control over is you.

When you feel the need to control your circumstance or other people, remember:

"TRUST IN THE LORD WITH ALL YOUR HEART AND LEAN NOT ON YOUR OWN UNDERSTANDING; IN ALL YOUR WAYS SUBMIT TO HIM, AND HE WILL MAKE YOUR PATHS STRAIGHT."
—PROVERB 3:5–6

For example, say you're standing in a line that's moving too slowly and you're becoming more and more anxious about the time it's taking. You specifically chose this line because it was the shortest and seemed to be moving the fastest. You've got to be somewhere in fifteen minutes and you're going to be late.

The clerk all of a sudden has problems with an item and needs to call the manager. You can't believe it. How could this happen to you? Why can't people learn to do their jobs?

You glance around to see if you can get into another line, but by now, they're all backed up. Isn't that just the way it goes? You look around, sigh, scowl at the person in front of you, fidget and shift your purchases, and mutter under your breath about general incompetence.

How many things in that scenario did you actually have control over?

- You didn't have any control over how fast the line moved.

- You didn't have any control over the problem with the item.

- You didn't have any control over what else the manager had to do before she could come over.

- You had control over the line you chose; that's about it.

Anxiety seeks to personalize and control, as a way to manage the pain and distress. These strategies, however, don't decrease pain and distress; they add to them by turning everyday occurrences into disasters.

## The Perils of Perfectionism

What was the source of the anxiety?

- Was it really the line? No, it was how long the line was taking.

- The anxiety stemmed from the thought of being late.

This is the perfectionist mindset creeping in. You decide in your anxiety that you must not be late, but who decided it was a disaster to be late? Anxiety speaks in the language of absolutes. Anxiety says you must not be late, but things happen in life all the time that mess up our timing.

Right-sizing the small stuff means accepting that small stuff exists, life happens, and your misery is not the sole purpose of the universe. To right-size the small stuff you need to learn to let the small stuff be small stuff.

**ANXIETY SPEAKS IN THE LANGUAGE OF ABSOLUTES. RIGHT-SIZE THE SMALL STUFF.**

Instead of fighting the small stuff, factor in the small stuff. Once that happens, letting go of the small stuff becomes much easier. Letting go of the small stuff is important because of how much small stuff life seems to have.

Anxious people tend to hold on to everything, both great and small, and have a difficult time letting anything go. If you hold on to every little slight, every little bobble, every little hiccup, every little dip or swerve in the road of life, you're going to run out of hands. Anxiety will tell you that you must hold on to all of these things to control your anxiety. Anxiety says controlling all of these things will bring you greater safety, but that's not true.

- The more things you hang on to, the more things you seek to control.

- The more things you seek to control, the more things you feel compelled to defend.

- The more things you feel compelled to defend, the more your life feels like it's under attack and the more anxious you become.

## Life and Its Terms

The recovery community—Alcoholics Anonymous in particular—seems to have a handle on the futility of attempting to control what cannot be controlled. One of their mantras is learning to accept life on life's terms. Life's terms include days of dealing with the small stuff.

Another mainstay of the recovery community is a saying credited to Reinhold Niebuhr, known as the Serenity Prayer. The prayer asks God for the serenity to accept what cannot be changed, the courage to change what can be changed, and the wisdom to know the difference between the two. So much in life cannot be changed, including random circumstance. Anxiety wants you to change what cannot be changed, stops you from changing what you can, and keeps you from recognizing the difference.

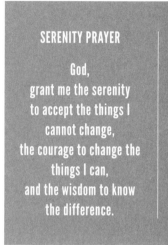

**SERENITY PRAYER**

God,
grant me the serenity
to accept the things I
cannot change,
the courage to change the
things I can,
and the wisdom to know
the difference.

## Declutter *Your* Anxieties

Anxiety, because it refuses to let anything go, is not unlike an emotional hoarder. Hoarders are anxious people, people who are anxious about letting certain things go, such as refusing to throw out receipts, newspapers, notes, mail, anything on paper. Their lives become so cluttered with all of these things that they find essential, they have difficulty functioning. Some hoarders have filled up their houses to the point of danger and sleep in their cars, until those too become filled to the point of danger.

Anxiety is a negativity hoarder, refusing to let go of any disparaging thought, potential terror, or possible disaster. Anxiety refuses to see the danger of the negativity it produces and panics at the thought of giving up hidden assumptions and mistaken beliefs. By refusing to let go of the small stuff, anxiety really majors in the minors.

**BEING ANXIOUS IS A HUMAN TRAIT. STAYING ANXIOUS IS A TERRIBLE WAY TO LIVE.**

Right-sizing the small stuff requires decluttering your anxieties. Anxiety clutter is all those assumptions and beliefs you hang on to because you mistakenly think they're true. The next time life hits you with some small stuff and you become anxious, take time to pay attention to what you say to yourself.

- Why are you so anxious?

- What are you worried about?

- What are you sure is going to happen?

Start seeing these hidden assumptions and mistaken beliefs for what they are: anxiety clutter. The more you have to worry about, the more you'll worry.

Anxiety will try to convince you that you're not a hoarder but a collector. Anxiety will try to tell you that your anxieties are really treasures to be protected, because they are valuable. Don't listen. Being anxious is a human trait and understandable. Staying anxious is a terrible way to live.

Jesus, in the Sermon on the Mount, gave his own instruction on living life on life's terms. He said not to worry about tomorrow because tomorrow would worry about itself. He also understood the nature of small stuff when he went on to say that each day has enough trouble of its own: "Therefore do not worry about tomorrow, for tomorrow will worry about itself. Each day has enough trouble of its own" (Matthew 6:34).

How difficult Jesus' instructions are to carry out! Don't we find ourselves constantly worrying not only about today but also about tomorrow? Instead of living each day as it comes, we pile worry on top of worry, day after day after day!

Jesus did not want us to be anxiety hoarders. Instead, he instructed us to leave worry behind and to seek first his kingdom and his righteousness. Anxiety is not only a hoarder, it is also a jealous hoarder. Anxiety wants to monopolize all of your time and energy in worry and fear, leaving you little time to concentrate on the blessings and promises of God. Anxiety seeks to rob you of your peace and trust in God. No wonder Jesus warned us against it!

# Work *at* Not Working

"**Why** can't you just relax?" Jason asked, exasperated. He'd planned a morning at the park with the kids and then lunch at their favorite neighborhood eatery. Hannah was quick to say, as usual, no, she couldn't go, because she had too much work to do.

"Look, the house isn't that bad. Just come with us, and after lunch, we'll all pitch in to help," Jason said, trying a different tactic.

"Right," Hannah responded sarcastically. "We can let the four-year-old clean the bathroom." There was one way to clean the house, and Hannah was the only one who understood why that way was important and necessary.

Admitting defeat, Jason gathered up the crew and trooped out the door. The kids were chatting excitedly to each other, the oldest yelling out a distracted good-bye to Hannah. None of them bothered to ask if she was going along, because she never did.

Seething, Hannah marched into the kitchen to start work. Fine for them to go off and play, but Saturday was a workday. Somebody in the family needed to be responsible.

Besides, Jason never seemed to know what to do, and the kids made cleaning the house worse. They always managed to come in right behind her and mess up whatever she'd just cleaned. Hannah lived for that one brief moment when the house was finally clean and quiet, when she could look around and feel that all was right with her world—at least until the front door opened. She worked so hard to get everything right, but things never stayed that way.

Tense and resentful, Hannah started to clean; she couldn't stand the way the house was one more minute.

■ ■ ■

Anxiety and relaxation are polar opposites. Anxious people rarely relax. Some anxious people, like Hannah, deal with their anxiety through a whirlwind of activities and tasks. Other anxious people deal with their anxiety by engaging in distracting activities, such as watching television or playing video games. They may talk and text on the phone or even read. At first glance, some might appear to be relaxing, but a closer look reveals an edge, a drive to their activities that prevents real relaxation. Try interrupting one of these activities and you'll find out just how "relaxed" they are.

The body has to sleep and will do so, of its own accord, whether a person wants to or not. Relaxation, however, is not an automatic response. Some people come by relaxation quite naturally, but I have found that relaxation is a skill anxious people need to learn.

## At-Ease

Have you ever seen the guards at Buckingham Palace in London? They are the ones who stand ramrod straight, eyes focused ahead, for hours and hours. Of course, there are tourists who attempt to distract them from their duty, but these soldiers remain rigidly vigil. Similarly, anxiety remains rigidly vigil and rarely issues the order "At ease."

In order to truly relax, you need to recognize that you are in control of your life. You don't need to get up and report to anxiety for duty. You have the power within yourself to stand down from anxiety and relax.

Anxious people are often skeptical of this power. When asked about the ability to relax, the anxious person will often say, "I can't relax." They will back up that statement with a long list of reasons why relaxation is impossible. These reasons are most often credited to outside circumstances or other people. The idea of having the power to relax, regardless of circumstances or the actions of others, is a foreign concept to anxious people. The thought that when they say "I cannot," they really mean "I will not" is difficult to accept.

## Safety Counts

Anxieties demand that relaxation is only possible when the person is "safe." Like a dangled carrot, safety seems always just out of reach. Safety is always out of reach because, for the anxious, safety does not come from what is happening around the person but from what is happening inside the person. An anxious person rarely feels safe, no matter the outside circumstances.

This is the false promise and the paradox of anxiety: anxiety says you are safe when you feel safe, but because you never feel safe, you never are safe. Never safe, you never truly relax.

Again, feeling safe and being safe are two different things. Being safe is an objective conclusion. Feeling safe is a subjective opinion.

Hannah felt she couldn't relax until her house was completely clean to her standards. Untidy, to Hannah, meant unsafe. Was Hannah unsafe in a house with dishes left in the sink? Objectively no, but subjectively yes. Hannah prioritized her feelings of unsafety over spending family time with her children and husband. A messy house didn't put Hannah in any danger, but rejecting her family did, because her rejection jeopardized those vital relationships.

> True safety comes from trusting God.
>
> "FEAR OF MAN WILL PROVE TO BE A SNARE, BUT WHOEVER TRUSTS IN THE LORD IS KEPT SAFE."
> —PROVERBS 29:25

## Contentment Commitment

If you're holding out until the conditions are just right to relax, you may find you never relax. Unable to relax, you may find you are never satisfied with your state of being. If you can't be satisfied, you cannot be content. I think relaxation and contentment are a matched pair. When a person is content, then the door is opened wide for true relaxation.

**CONTENTMENT IS A SKILL THAT CAN BE LEARNED.**

Anxious people could learn a thing or two about contentment from the apostle Paul. In his letter to the Philippians, he made an astonishing statement. He said he had "learned to be content whatever the circumstances" (Philippians 4:11). Paul said that in any situation, he could find contentment, whether in need or in plenty, well fed or hungry, because of the strength he had through Christ (Philippians 4:12–13).

The apostle Paul learned how to be content whatever his circumstances—and, remember, in 2 Corinthians 11:23–28 he listed some of those circumstances:

- working hard
- in prison
- flogged
- in danger of his life

- beaten; pelted with stones
- shipwrecked
- adrift in the sea
- moving from place to place
- in danger from rivers, bandits, other people
- in danger in the city and in the country
- long days and sleepless nights
- hungry, thirsty, cold, and naked
- concerned about his ministry and work

If he could learn, through all of that, to find contentment, shouldn't we be able to learn to find contentment and relaxation, even given the pressures of our lives?

I like that Paul said he "learned." I feel better because that means Paul wasn't one of those people who are naturally content. This also means that contentment—and I would argue relaxation—is a skill that can be learned. No more of this "I can't." Instead, you need to admit, "I can, but I don't know how"; and further, "I don't know how, but I can learn." Anxieties are dead-end thinkers; you must become a possibility thinker.

Now is the time to give yourself permission to assign relaxation a place in your life. Learning to relax means you will initially need to work at not working. Again, this will not feel natural at first. You may find yourself constantly popping up, scurrying off—either mentally or physically—to take care of some worry, only to stop and tell yourself to, in essence, sit back down!

Tell fear no, so you can tell relaxation yes. Stop listening to all the reasons you can't or shouldn't, and remind yourself of the reasons you can and should.

## Relaxation 101

You need to accept that relaxation is going to feel strange. Relaxation may even feel unsafe. As I talked about earlier, you need to analyze those thoughts and figure out which ones are subjective and which ones are objective. The sky is not going to fall if you sit down and relax. You don't have to earn the right to relax.

Start small. Pick out one or two things you would like to do to relax. This could be sitting down with a cup of hot tea or taking a short walk or reading a favorite book (you could always choose the Bible). You might stop long enough to pet your cat, play with your dog, read a book with your child. From this short list, give yourself permission to do one of these a day. As you start to do this, turn up the volume and pay attention to the messages anxiety will begin to broadcast. Write them down for later; now is the time to relax!

Here are some other skills you can learn to assist with relaxation:

## ■ CONTROLLED BREATHING

Anxieties often start in the mind and fast-forward to the body, resulting in rapid breathing, or hyperventilation. When you hyperventilate, you take in more oxygen than you need. Your ratio of oxygen to carbon dioxide gets unbalanced, resulting in increased heart rate, tingling in your extremities, and feeling light-headed. Paradoxically, when you hyperventilate, you can feel like you're not getting enough air, that you're suffocating, so you try to breathe even faster. Some people in the midst of this kind of an anxiety-propelled cycle can pass out, which is your body's way of trying to reestablish order.

When anxious, your breathing can cycle out of control. But you can learn how to take back control of your breathing. There are several types of these breathing techniques, but the one that seems the simplest to me is called foursquare breathing:

1. Breathe in on a count of four.

2. Hold your breath for a count of four.

3. Exhale over a count of four.

4. Wait and do not breathe in for a count of four.

The first time you use this technique, do it ten times, breathing slower and deeper each time.

## ■ FIND YOUR HAPPY PLACE

This relaxation technique involves a quick mental getaway without ever leaving. Your mind goes elsewhere, only this time to a happy place, while your body stays put.

1. Find a quiet place.

2. Close your eyes and imagine a peaceful place, one where you feel comfortable.

3. Breathe deeply and slowly.

4. Imagine what this place looks like, feels like, smells like, and sounds like. Mentally explore this quiet place, using your imagination.

If you're able, listen to relaxing music or natural sounds: waves on a beach, rain in a forest, wind blowing, or the sound of birds. Make sure to keep this volume turned down softly. Work toward staying in this relaxed state for about ten minutes.

## ROLLING RELAXATION

You can do this either sitting up or lying down. Start with either the top of your head or the bottom of your feet, and tighten each muscle group as you travel either down or up your body. Hold the tension for three to five seconds; then release the tension and move to the next part of your body.

There aren't any more "rules" for this. Try finding what works best for you. When you have gone through your entire body, remain relaxed for several minutes. You could even use your happy-place music or sounds and incorporate both of these together; engage in rolling relaxation and finish with a trip to your happy place.

## LIFE UNPLUGGED

Our days are awash in noise. Some anxious people use the white noise of life as a way to drown out their negative inner voices. Peace and quiet becomes anything but. One of the ways for you to learn to relax is to reacquaint yourself with the joy of quiet. Anxieties will want to come rushing into that void, but you must resist that temptation.

While enjoying the quiet, practice controlled breathing. Use the soft sounds of your breathing, along with the intervening times of quiet. If you find staying still difficult to accomplish, try taking a walk unplugged. Not only detach from anything that plugs into your ears, but also detach from what keeps plugging into your mind. Instead, fill your thoughts with the beauty around you, paying attention not to what you're hearing but to what you're seeing.

■ WORK OUT TO RELAX

There are many ways to engage your body energetically enough to quiet your mind. Walking is a great way to move your body, while you relax your mind. I've been a runner for years and find the physical exertion one of the best things I do to relax each day. You might want to play on a team (composed, I hope, of positive people), swim, bike, or go to a nearby gym. Before you embark on a higher level of exercise, however, take time to check in with your primary care physician to get an objective assessment of the proper level of exercise for your physical condition.

Anxiety can be a tyrant where sleep is concerned. Being anxious, you may find yourself constantly keyed up yet exhausted at the same time. You might find yourself able to fall asleep but experience difficulty staying asleep. Lack of sleep is debilitating mentally and physically, so restful sleep is critical to well-being. Here are a few tips for a restful night:

- Keep to a regular sleep schedule. Allow your body to establish a healthy sleep routine, and don't vary it by more than an hour one way or the other each night.

- Have the room where you sleep dark, quiet, well ventilated, and a comfortable temperature. Use a supportive, comfortable bed.

- Avoid tobacco products.

- Avoid alcohol right before bed.

- Keep your bedroom a bedroom: don't have in it any distractions like a work space, a television, or a computer.

- If you have trouble sleeping, try drinking a small glass of warm milk before going to bed.

- Turn your clock around, so you can't see it and won't spend time wondering what time it is.

- Take a hot bath or shower just before bed.

- Use one of the earlier relaxation techniques.

- Pray.

Maybe that last suggestion should have been the first suggestion. The more time you've spent giving in to anxiety, the more help you'll need saying no. Prayer is an excellent avenue for such help. In *The Message*, Eugene Peterson phrases Luke 12:29 like this:

> What I'm trying to do here is get you to relax, not be so preoccupied with *getting* so you can respond to God's *giving*. People who don't know God and the way he works fuss over these things, but you know both God and how he works. Steep yourself in God-reality, God-initiative, God-provisions. You'll find all your everyday human concerns will be met. Don't be afraid of missing out. You're my dearest friends! The Father wants to give you the very kingdom itself.

Each night when you lay down and each morning when you get up, realign yourself with God's plan and purpose for you, and tell anxiety to take a hike!

# Take Baby Steps

*Dan* could remember, like it was yesterday, when his life started closing in on itself. That stupid sales call that hadn't resulted in anything positive. He'd been driving in an unfamiliar part of town. The weather was lousy—rain with terrible visibility. He'd barely realized he was in a tunnel when the wash of red brake lights blossomed in front of him, reflecting off of the tiled walls. Slamming on the brakes, he'd barely stopped in time. Construction had backed everything up.

Stuck in that dingy, soot-covered tunnel, his initial panic hadn't gone away. As he waited for the traffic to move, it seemed like the walls were curving in on him. He started to sweat and could feel his heart thumping away. That was the first time he'd thought he was having a heart attack. It wouldn't be the last.

Terrified of feeling that way again, Dan never did go back to that potential customer. He became claustrophobic and started avoiding tunnels. It got to the point where driving itself was difficult. His sales plummeted as he began to make excuses for why he was no longer able to do his job. Losing that job was almost a relief, but after almost two years, he hadn't gotten another one. The panic attacks kept coming until even his house was no longer a safe place.

■ ■ ■

I remember working with a woman who, like Dan, experienced a panic attack out of the blue—in a Seattle elevator. For those of you who are familiar with Seattle, no, it wasn't on the glass elevator on the outside of the Space Needle. This was just a normal elevator in a downtown high-rise. She'd been worried about a pivotal presentation she had been headed to when she'd heard a thunk and a grinding noise. Already stressed out, she went into full-blown panic mode, sure she was about to plummet to her death.

Nothing happened to the elevator, which kept going as usual, but she did not. From that point on, until she came in for counseling, she refused to ride another elevator. Even climbing stairs produced thoughts of anxiety.

Dan's issue appeared to be first tunnels, then driving. Her issue appeared to be first elevators, then heights. The real issue for each of them was the panic attack— that ambush of terror where each was convinced that they were about to die. In order to avoid ever feeling that way again, each sought to control and avoid duplicating their conditions. They both sought to control the externals when the problem was internal.

Both experienced a progression in their fears. Each started by being afraid of a specific event. That initial fear transferred to becoming fearful of being fearful, for any reason. Both become hypervigilant to the state of their feelings. Were they anxious? Were they afraid? Had they started to hyperventilate? Were their hearts pounding? Did they suddenly feel disconnected from the present moment? Was it happening again?

## One Rung *at a* Time

Anxieties are progressive, so it seems logical that one of the answers to anxiety would be a progression of a different kind. When a fear starts out small and keeps expanding, the way to combat anxiety is to cut that anxiety down to size. Instead of trying to take on the

whole fear, you start small, working your way up your fear, like climbing a ladder. As you become comfortable at each rung of your fear, you become ready to climb up to the next.

For Dan, the first rung of his fear ladder was physically getting back into his car. After all, his car was the location of that first panic attack. Once the first rung of getting into his car was accomplished, the next rung was starting his car. After that, it was driving his car. Rung by rung by rung, he worked at becoming comfortable again driving to known places.

When those no longer produced a sense of panic, Dan was ready to drive an unfamiliar route in the daytime, then at night. Rung by rung by rung. At each step, he turned up the volume, evaluated the fear, and differentiated between the objective and subjective perspectives.

Take heart! You belong to God and he has promised to help you.

"MY GOD WILL MEET ALL YOUR NEEDS ACCORDING TO THE RICHES OF HIS GLORY IN CHRIST JESUS."
—PHILIPPIANS 4:19

"HIS DIVINE POWER HAS GIVEN US EVERYTHING WE NEED FOR A GODLY LIFE THROUGH OUR KNOWLEDGE OF HIM WHO CALLED US BY HIS OWN GLORY AND GOODNESS."
—2 PETER 1:3

For the woman I worked with, her first rung was looking at pictures of office buildings as we evaluated her discomfort. The next rung was walking around a few of those high-rise buildings in person. The next rung was entering and exiting just the lobbies. Then we started going up and down small flights of stairs in short buildings. Next we moved to going up and down small flights of stairs in tall buildings.

One of the biggest rungs was getting on and off an elevator at the ground floor. We didn't go up at first, just in and out the door. The next rung was going up one floor, getting off, walking a few yards, getting back on the elevator, and riding down. Rung by rung by rung. Step by step by step. Along the way, we utilized breathing and relaxation techniques, taking time to work through the process.

## Defining Desensitization

This progressive exposure is also called *desensitization*. I've also often referred to this as baby steps. Taking on a full-fledged fear in its immensity is simply too big a task when you're in the throes of anxiety. Instead, taking on small, bite-sized pieces of that fear is just enough to allow for progress. Each successful rung on the fear ladder, each baby step taken, provides momentum and courage to go on to the next.

This rung-by-rung, step-by-step progression works well with fears because fears are generally made of smaller, interconnected components. Fears are like a geodesic dome—a large structure being supported by a series of small, interlocking parts. Deconstruct the parts and the fear crumbles like a house-of-cards.

### ■ START SMALL

Desensitization means starting small. If you become overly anxious at being in a crowd, start small—literally—with a small group of people. Start with people you know and like, learning to be comfortable with them in a safe, social setting, such as your home. Next try going with that same group of people to a different setting, such as to a restaurant or movie or go to an outside event.

### ■ ASK FOR HELP

Some people are able to work up the rungs of desensitization on their own, but others find working with a counselor helpful. At each step, work through your fears, identifying them, acknowledging them, and challenging them. If you've made progress on your own but then find yourself stymied, unable to move forward, don't be afraid to ask for help. A trusted friend, faith advisor, family member, or counselor can often provide the third-party perspective needed to deconstruct the fear barrier.

## ■ PRACTICE

As you encounter and conquer smaller fear situations, begin to integrate those experiences into your daily routine. Don't just go out once to dinner or a movie with friends just to prove you can; work this activity into your life going forward. Practice, practice, practice!

## ■ USE YOUR TOOLS

As you progress through desensitization, don't forget you have tools at your disposal to help work past the fear. Controlled breathing, for example, can give you back control over the hyperventilation so prevalent in anxiety. Talk back to your anxiety and remind yourself of what is true. Don't allow fear to dominate your inner dialogue.

## ■ KEEP TRYING

Celebrate each victory as you walk the baby steps toward relief from anxiety. Shame and blame may attempt to derail your progress, but don't listen! If you get stuck at a certain level and experience "failure," that is not a reason to give up. Each setback holds the key to future success, if you'll objectively look at what happened, seek to understand why, and find a way to try, try again.

## IDENTIFY THE NEXT STEP

As you successfully climb each rung, stop and celebrate your victory but also identify your next baby step. The goal is progress. As you desensitize yourself to your anxiety, you'll also be reacquainting yourself with progress, accomplishment, and empowerment.

## REFUSE TO GIVE UP

Don't be surprised if along the way you are emboldened to take a giant leap but fall flat on your face. It happens. Overcoming anxiety isn't a race. The goal is progress. Anxiety wants you to stay firmly stuck, with fear calling the shots. By refusing to give up, you inch step by step toward reclaiming control over your life.

## ■ KNOW THAT YOU ARE WORTH THE EFFORT

Along this journey to overcoming anxiety, facing fear in the face, and claiming victory, you will learn a great deal about yourself. You may even learn to appreciate yourself—to love yourself—better than you do now. You deserve more than a life riddled with anxiety and fear. You are more than that monster.

## ■ CHRONICLE YOUR JOURNEY

I always like to recommend that people chronicle this important journey of self-discovery. You might write down significant moments in a journal. You might find small tokens at critical points along the way to remind you of your progress. Those who encounter recovery through Alcoholics Anonymous and other self-help groups use tokens—small coins in the case of AA—to great effect.

# Take *Your* First Step

The only way to *take* baby steps is to take baby steps. You can think about baby steps. You can visualize baby steps. You can argue all you want for baby steps. But you will never go anywhere until you *take* a baby step.

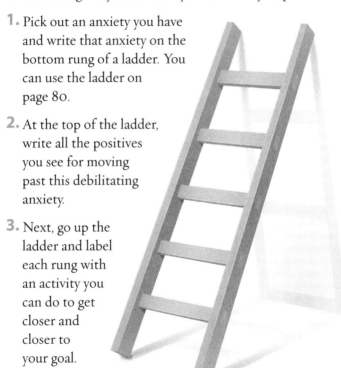

1. Pick out an anxiety you have and write that anxiety on the bottom rung of a ladder. You can use the ladder on page 80.

2. At the top of the ladder, write all the positives you see for moving past this debilitating anxiety.

3. Next, go up the ladder and label each rung with an activity you can do to get closer and closer to your goal.

Determine if you can take the first step alone or if you need to call in reinforcements. If you don't think you can take the step yourself, the first rung is to identify who can help and then to contact that person. Be honest. You have no way to know what benefit that other person will receive by participating in this journey you're taking. I know I have been personally blessed to watch the courage and progress of others. It strengthens my faith and gives me courage to conquer my own anxieties.

Lastly, don't forget you have a loving Father who is all-for your baby steps. His desire is for you to take those steps, so you can get up to speed on the plans he has for your life! Here are a few Scriptures specifically about taking steps that I thought would be helpful for you to know—even to memorize—or turn into active, personal prayers:

- ■ "My steps have held to your paths; my feet have not stumbled."—Psalm 17:5

- ■ "The LORD makes firm the steps of the one who delights in him."—Psalm 37:23

- ■ "When you walk, your steps will not be hampered; when you run, you will not stumble." —Proverbs 4:12

- "The simple believe anything, but the prudent give thought to their steps."—Proverbs 14:15

- "In their hearts humans plan their course, but the Lord establishes their steps."—Proverbs 16:9

- "To this you were called . . . that you should follow in his steps."—1 Peter 2:21

You were called to follow in Christ's steps, to live out a life according to God's calling. Anxiety and fear keep you trapped, ever yearning but never realizing the hope-filled plans God has for you. God is for you as you take those baby steps toward freedom!

# Make Healthy Choices

*Did* you ever play with wind-up toys as a kid? Remember how if you wound the toy too far, it broke? Well, you are the wind-up toy. You are the wind-up toy, and anxiety keeps winding and winding you up. At some point, anxiety could over-wind you, so you'll break. You'll break emotionally, you'll break spiritually, and you'll break physically. Ironically, when we wind *up*, we break *down*.

Anxiety puts your body into high gear. When you're supposed to be idling or even stopped, anxiety is revving your physical engine. When the light turns green, you've revved up so high that you shoot into the intersection of life, charged up and not always looking where you're going.

Because you're revving at such a high speed, you've got to slam on the brakes hard if you need to stop. Sometimes, you find you can't stop, and you run into things and people you shouldn't.

With anxiety constantly gunning your motor, you find you get lousy gas mileage. Anxiety is putting so much wear and tear on your body that at some point, the engine's going to fall out.

■ ■ ■

You, of course, are not really a car, but your body is an intricate and beautifully made flesh-and-blood machine. When anxiety is in the driver's seat of your life, that machine is bound to be overworked and overwrought. When there is no peace, your anxiety is always on the move, forcing the machine of your body to work, work, work.

Revved up, your body doesn't get the time it needs to

stand down, to relax, to rebuild itself, as God designed. Right after telling us to stop worrying, Jesus, in the Sermon on the Mount, asked this question: "Can any of you by worrying add a single hour to your life?" (Matthew 6:27). This was a rhetorical question, and Jesus did not intend for anyone to answer that question yes.

But isn't that how anxiety answers that question? Anxiety says worrying is necessary in order to keep track of all of the potential dangers and problems and catastrophes just lurking around the corner. Anxiety says all of these things must be worried about and tracked, not only to ensure an additional hour, but maybe even an additional day or month or year!

**WE CAN EITHER TRUST GOD OR WE CAN TRUST ANXIETY.**

Jesus is right and anxiety is wrong. Jesus says stop worrying and let tomorrow worry about itself. James echoes this: "Why, you do not even know what will happen tomorrow" (James 4:14). Therein lies the secret of anxiety. We don't really know what will happen tomorrow. Within that void of knowledge, we have a choice. We can either trust God, or we can trust anxiety which says we may not know what will happen tomorrow but we do know it will be bad.

Anxiety, as I've said before, puts people on the alert. That alert is lived out through physical responses. The engine of the body is constantly revving, using up fuel and physical resources, creating emotional and physical depletion.

## Fill *the* Tank

Anxiety already takes a toll on the body. The toll is like a car being asked to pull an oversized trailer up a steep hill. The cheaper the grade of fuel—the lower the level of octane—the greater the chance you'll end up pulled off to the side of the road, overstretched and overheated.

Your body is like a car. When you combine a heavy physical load with low-grade fuel, you're bound to have problems. You'll never make it up that hill without breaking down. Even on the straightaways, you'll wheeze and smoke and sputter.

As you work to reduce the strain that anxiety puts on the engine of your body, start filling your tank with the right kind of fuel. With the right fuel, you'll be able to operate at a better physical level, even as you wind down from the stress and strain of anxiety. Be aware, however, that your definition of the right kind of fuel and mine might be very different.

Over the years, as I've worked with highly anxious people, I've noticed enough of a trend to mention. Often, when anxious people pull into the gas station, they choose the convenient packaged and processed foods as fuel, topped off with a supercharged dose of caffeine. This get-charged-quick diet seems tailor-made for their over-revved-up life.

This fuel may provide that quick burst of energy, but at what price? A few hours after the fuel-up, the bottom drops out and you can forget about going another step, let alone up another hill. The yo-yo affect this fueling produces often matches the up-and-down, feast-or-famine, supercharged and drop-to-the-bottom mood swings of anxiety from catastrophe to apathy and back again.

# Make Healthy Choices

A vital answer to anxiety, then, is making healthy choices about what you eat and drink. I realize I'm going to sound like a broken record (or even your mother), but eating healthy is not rocket science. Eating healthy is, however, an intentional activity. *You*—not *anxiety*—must choose the types of food and drink best able to fortify and strengthen you physically as you heal from the ravages of anxiety.

## ■ WHOLE FOODS

When fueling up for your life, you need to overwhelmingly choose whole foods, not processed foods. Whole foods are those found, generally, on the outside ring of grocery stores: fresh vegetables and fruit, whole-grain breads and pasta, lean meats, fish, and dairy products.

## ■ HEALTHY FATS

Fats have gotten a bad reputation, but not all fats are bad. There are good fats from sources like fish, flaxseed, and olive oil. Your body was designed to need a small amount of good fat to operate optimally.

## ■ NUTRITIONAL SUPPLEMENTS

When the body is stressed out physically because of anxiety, nutrients are depleted. A well-rounded multivitamin that includes vitamins, minerals, and amino acids is key to providing the components needed for health.

## ■ REAL INGREDIENTS

There are people with real sensitivities and allergies to many of the artificial ingredients used in food processing. These sensitivities and allergies can lie under the surface, causing physical problems without revealing their source. Pay attention to the ingredient label on every food you buy and eat. When the ingredients become a string of unpronounceable syllables, that's when you may want to put the package down and head for the produce aisle.

## ■ INCREASE WATER

Water is vital to healthy physical functioning. Our bodies are predominantly composed of water, including our muscles and our brains. We use water to digest our food and absorb nutrients. Water detoxifies the kidneys and liver and helps our bodies eliminate waste. If water sounds boring to you, you can add to it all kinds of fruits and flavors and even vitamin and nutrient packets.

## ■ DECREASE CAFFEINE

I like coffee. I drink coffee, so I'm not going to say, "No coffee or caffeine." However, there are people who practically live on coffee and caffeine drinks. A moderate amount of caffeine helps you stay alert. An excessive amount of caffeine helps you stay anxious. In addition, caffeine is a diuretic, which can lead to dehydration.

## ■ HEALTHY WEIGHT

Each person is an individual with a range of what constitutes a healthy weight. Too little weight and the body is stressed. Too much weight and the body is stressed. When you find that middle ground where health is found and disordered eating is absent, you've located that healthy weight. Finding that healthy weight, however, isn't always easy, so I suggest working with a healthcare provider who can become a coach and health advocate.

## ■ A SPRINKLE OF SUGAR

Sugar is a high-octane, potent, mood-altering fuel. In other words, a little goes a long way. Large amounts spike your blood levels, sending you on a roller-coaster ride of jittery highs and crashing lows. When you add caffeine into this mix, the result is compounded. You don't need to say "Never" to sugar, but most of us could learn to say "Not so much" more often.

## ■ CHILL OUT

Anxious people have a tendency to, well, become anxious. Food anxieties are very real, with people becoming terrified to eat this or that for overblown or imagined consequences. The point of eating healthy is not to produce increased anxiety about what you're eating! Don't let anxiety take up residence in your fridge or pantry.

## ■ MOVE

Your body was made to move, to engage in physical activity. Getting your body to move is a wonderful way to burn off nervous energy while increasing health, stamina, and strength.

Find a way each day for your body to move.

- Take a walk.

- Use the stairs, instead of the elevator.

- Park your car farther from work.

- Work in your garden.

- Get off a stop or two early from the bus or train.

- Check out your local recreation district for fitness classes.

- Join a neighborhood gym.

The ways are many, but remember, so are the excuses. Be objective about exercise, not subjective. Recognize its benefits and hold on to those while you lace up your sneakers.

When you place anxiety in the driver's seat, your body gets dragged along for the ride. Anxiety is pushing your body harder and harder, degrading your health and the quality of your life. As you work toward containing and controlling your anxiety, don't forget your body. Adjusting your lifestyle choices toward health can go a long way toward assisting your body to recover from anxiety.

Your body is in this fight toward recovery right along with your mind and soul. For many of you, these changes are hard. You may have used some unhealthy strategies to cope with your anxiety and will find it difficult to give those up. I understand.

If you are stuck between what you know you should do and what you're actually doing, again, call in reinforcements. Seek out encouragers in your life to help motivate you and keep you accountable. Seek out professional guidance and help if your physical health is a challenge.

You cannot disconnect your physical health from your emotional health and your spiritual health. When you deplete your body physically and do not give your body the proper fuel it needs to repair itself and run well, your heart, mind, and soul will suffer. When you make positive, healthy changes, your heart, mind, and soul benefit.

# Write *Your* Script

*As* Connie was going through her work email, she saw a meeting reminder added to her calendar. In two days, she was supposed to meet with her supervisor. Immediately, she felt that familiar jolt of panic.

What was the meeting about?
Why hadn't her supervisor told her about the meeting?
Was something wrong?
Did she do something wrong?

She started frantically reviewing the past several weeks to see if there had been any indication she'd messed up somewhere.

*Stop*, she finally told herself, as her heart raced and her breathing quickened. *You don't know anything is wrong. Just email her and ask for clarification.*

It turned out Connie's supervisor wanted her input on a potential software purchase. She'd meant to send an email to Connie explaining about the meeting but got distracted and simply forgot. No disaster, no catastrophe. Business as usual. Connie's response, however, had been anything but business as usual. This time, however, Connie stopped anxiety in its tracks. Taking a deep breath, holding it for a moment before letting it out slowly, Connie decided it was going to be a good day.

When Connie got that meeting reminder, anxiety tried to write an entire disaster script, starring the worst possible outcome. Connie's answer to anxiety was to yank that script out of anxiety's control, intentionally tear it up, and write her own script. She pushed pause on the panic button by objectively looking at the situation.

Instead of merely assuming the worst, Connie came up with a way to verify the reason for the meeting. Before, convinced by anxiety that the meeting was catastrophic, Connie would have avoided not only any mention of the meeting before it took place but also any contact with her supervisor. She might even have called in sick the day of the meeting. Not this time.

■ ■ ■

Anxieties yell "The sky is falling! The sky is falling!" when an acorn drops from a tree, in fits of panicked speculation. Just like the story of Chicken Little, the script anxiety writes doesn't have a happy ending. But another answer for anxiety is to fire anxiety from the script-writing business where your life is concerned. It's time to become your own, positive scriptwriter.

## *Your* World Stage

William Shakespeare may not be as widely read in this time of texts and tweets, but centuries later, his brilliance in writing about the human condition remains bright. In his play *As You Like It*, he wrote: "All the world's a stage, and all the men and women merely players: they have their exits and their entrances; and one man in his time plays many parts." Your life, in other words, is a play.

Within that play called life, you've allowed anxiety to act like a demanding diva. Anxiety has dictated the temperature of the room, the color of the M&M's®, the thread count of the sheets, and the number of shrimp in the salad. You've allowed anxiety to act like a dictating director. Anxiety has told you where to stand, what lines to say, when and where to move, and how to interact with others on the stage.

To take back your life, you need to stop taking direction from a tyrant and put yourself in charge of the script of your life. Anxiety has a dark, troubled, and foreboding script for you to follow. Refuse to play along. Yes, your life is a play, but you only have one performance. You must decide whose script you're going to follow.

## *The* Read-Through

What do actors do when they get a new script? In my limited theatrical experience, which happened far longer ago than I care to acknowledge, actors get together and do a read-through of the script. Sometimes, an actor is given the entire script and other times, an actor is given parts of the script, which are parceled out as the script is being written. I think the latter is more indicative of life. The scripts of our lives gets parceled out bit by bit, day by day, as events are happening.

When anxiety tries to slip in some of its doom-filled pages, stop and do a quick read-through. Determine what anxiety is trying to say. How does anxiety want you to act? Realize you are not obligated to follow anxiety's stage directions. Instead, put big, bold *X*s through anxiety's pages.

I've seen this technique used in a variety of ways over my tenure as a therapist. One of my favorite examples was of a woman I worked with who argued with herself like an opposing attorney. I'd think there was someone in the office with her, but she was arguing with herself out loud. She'd start reading out of anxiety's script and then substitute her own. She played devil's advocate with anxiety, all the while paying attention to the emotions each position stirred up in her.

> God's plans for your life are wildly better than anxiety's!
>
> "FOR I KNOW THE PLANS I HAVE FOR YOU," DECLARES THE LORD, "PLANS TO PROSPER YOU AND NOT TO HARM YOU, PLANS TO GIVE YOU HOPE AND A FUTURE."
> —JEREMIAH 29:11

There were times in the office (and I'm assuming at home) when she'd need to get out and take a walk, so her back-and-forth with herself wouldn't be so disruptive for others. I found it a novel way to work through issues. By the time she finished, she'd settled on the script that allowed her to stay positive and move forward in the situation.

Other people find it helpful to run these competing scripts past trusted friends or family. Anxiety has a script, and you are trying to develop a script that's different; but sometimes you can get confused as to which is correct. Especially with emotional or fearful situations, objectivity can be difficult to find. A third-party review can reassert an objective evaluation of both scripts. A third-party review can help you evaluate whether the script you're writing for yourself will likely produce the results you want. However you manage this, finding the right script for you and your situations is another answer to anxiety.

## Write *It* Out

Some people are auditory processors—they think with their mouths. Other people just aren't wired that way. If you're one of the latter types, I suggest actually writing out your script. You could write out your script by hand or on a computer. Journaling your story has great power, especially your struggles between the negatives and the positives at conflict within you. Each time you take time to chronicle a struggle, you contribute to the handbook of how to overcome and succeed the next time. In essence, you write your own self-help book.

Even if you don't consider yourself a writer, I encourage you to try journaling, just once. Consider this a baby step. You needn't write everything down in the moment, but you can choose a time—perhaps when things calm down—to write and reflect on your experience. Put aside any anxiety about penmanship or grammar. Put aside any anxiety about others reading what you've written or what you've written not being good enough. Put down anxiety and take that baby step!

Once you start the habit of writing your own script, I think you'll be surprised at the effect of this simple tool. If you've been reading from anxiety's script for a long time, you'll hear negativity in your head for a time. Hearing that voice doesn't mean you need to obey that voice. Once that negative script starts, you can, like Connie, stop it in its tracks and assert your own script, using your own voice.

Think about the type of character you've been playing with your anxiety as the director of your life. Then ask yourself the following question: Is that really the type of person you want to be?

Anxiety has written a script where you play the part of a frazzled, anxious, suspicious, irritable, short-tempered, and easily frustrated person. How would your life change if you could change the part you play into a character who is relaxed and not anxious, thoughtful and not reactive, seeing the good instead of pointing out the bad, approachable instead of putting up barriers? How do you want to be perceived by the other players on stage? When you take control of your own script, you determine the part you are going to play and then you act accordingly.

I think you will find that once you start changing your script and resetting your stage, others may find the freedom to change theirs. Every time friends or loved ones have stepped onto your stage in the past, they have entered a darkened, cluttered stage of fear, tripping and falling over your anxieties.

Not only will your stage be much more positive for you, but those who enter into your life will also find a much brighter place! Instead of being afraid of what you'll say or how you'll react, when you relax, others may relax. Instead of assuming you'll say no, others may regain the courage to ask to see if you'll say yes. You never know, but your courage to make such a radical and positive change may encourage someone else to do the same.

# Set *Your* Anchor

**We** started this journey with "Chicken Little," a fable told to children. It seems appropriate, then, that we should end with another story. This story, however, isn't a fable; it's a parable Jesus told, and it goes like this:

> Everyone who hears these words of mine and puts them into practice is like a wise man who built his house on the rock. The rain came down, the streams rose, and the winds blew and beat against that house; yet it did not fall, because it had its foundation on the rock. But everyone who hears these words of mine and does not put them into practice is like a foolish man who built his house on sand. The rain came down, the streams rose, and the winds blew and beat against that house, and it fell with a great crash (Matthew 7:24–27).

Although this parable might be beloved by children, this concept of anchoring is anything but childish. The apostle Paul uses a similar analogy when he argues for Christians to anchor to spiritual maturity. When we are anchored to God, Paul says, "Then we will no longer be infants, tossed back and forth by the waves, and blown here and there by every wind of teaching and by the cunning and craftiness of people in their deceitful scheming" (Ephesians 4:14).

The final answer to anxiety, then, is to firmly anchor your faith in the strong and mighty bedrock of God and his promises. Anxiety has kept you tethered to the sandy shores of worry, fear, doubt, and dread. When the storms of life hit, when the streams of circumstance rise, even a little, and when the winds of doubt buffet your mind, you crash and give in to panic. Jesus calls this foolishness.

Anxiety does not like to be called foolish. Anxiety likes to be called prudent and watchful and alert. Anxiety puffs itself up and claims that it is the opposite of foolishness, that its concerns are wise. Yet Jesus calls this type of anxious life foolish.

Perhaps Jesus would also say it is foolish to live a life of small faith.

A life of small faith is not the life God intends for you. "For the Spirit God gave us does not make us timid, but gives us power, love and self-discipline" (2 Timothy 1:7). Anxiety desires for you to cower in a corner, saying yes to anxiety and no to practically anything else. Anxiety seeks to rob you of power, while God, through his Spirit, seeks to give you power.

The time has come to:

- listen to God more than to your anxieties.

- place your trust in God and stop trusting your anxieties.

- grasp firmly the freedom God has promised through Christ: "Therefore, if anyone is in Christ, the new creation has come: The old has gone, the new is here!" (2 Corinthians 5:17).

## Trust God

The time has come to stop doubting God, as your anxieties demand. Be like the father whose son was healed by Jesus. Jesus pointed out this man's anxiety and doubt as to whether Jesus could really heal his son: "'Everything is possible for one who believes.' Immediately the boy's father exclaimed, 'I do believe; help me overcome my unbelief!'" (Mark 9:23–24). You can say as well, *I do believe; help me overcome my unbelief.*

Saying no to anxieties can be a scary activity. Anxieties appear to provide an answer, a way to know what the future will hold. Granted, that future is always negative, but at least that future is always known. The unknown can be frightening. For an anxiety, what is unknown will always be negative.

> "FOR NOW WE SEE ONLY A REFLECTION AS IN A MIRROR; THEN WE SHALL SEE FACE TO FACE. NOW I KNOW IN PART; THEN I SHALL KNOW FULLY, EVEN AS I AM FULLY KNOWN"
> —1 CORINTHIANS 13:12

But what does God say about the unknown? God says to wait and trust because, as the saying goes, while you may not know what the future holds, you know who holds the future. Again, the apostle Paul wrestled with the unknown and concluded: "For now we see only a reflection as in a mirror; then we shall see face to face. Now I know in part; then I shall know fully, even as I am fully known" (1 Corinthians 13:12).

You do not know what tomorrow will bring, and nothing you can do will reveal that knowledge to you.

- Proverbs 27:1 says, "Do not boast about tomorrow, for you do not know what a day may bring."

- James says, "Why, you do not even know what will happen tomorrow" (James 4:14).

Anxieties boast that they know about tomorrow, but they do not. Only God knows what tomorrow may bring you—or if you'll even have a tomorrow. I suppose that is why Jesus said, "Therefore do not worry about tomorrow, for tomorrow will worry about itself. Each day has enough trouble of its own" (Matthew 6:34).

**YOUR FEARS CANNOT SAVE YOU; ONLY GOD CAN.**

Your fears cannot save you; only God can. When you choose to align yourself with your fears, you move farther from God.

Make no mistake; your anxieties will fight hard to retain control. As you begin to surrender your trust more and more to God and his promises, the less and less your anxieties will be happy. They will scream and wail and throw a temper tantrum for attention.

This is the time for prayer. "Do not be anxious about anything, but in every situation, by prayer and petition, with thanksgiving, present your requests to God" (Philippians 4:6). The apostle Paul did not say you could hold on to *some* anxieties; he said don't be anxious about *anything*. He did not say you could be anxious in *some* situations, he said you weren't to be anxious in *every* situation. That is a tall order!

## Pray *and* Petition

So how do you pull off such a miracle, if you've been an anxious person for as long as you can remember? The apostle Paul says you don't pull this off at all. Rather, the ability to know this kind of peace is the work of God through his Holy Spirit.

When faced with anxious situations, Paul says to pray and to petition. By petitioning, you explain to God what you want, what you need, and why. By praying, you open yourself up to his Spirit, to work with and through you to bring your requests to God.

What is the outcome of this prayer and petition? "The peace of God, which transcends all understanding, will guard your hearts and your minds in Christ Jesus (Philippians 4:7). This verse does not say "might" or "may" or "could." This verse says "will." This verse is a promise of God.

Anxieties, as I said before, try to present themselves as wise and prudent. Not being anxious, they will tell you, is foolish and dangerous; yet, by surrendering your anxieties to God, you gain peace. Paul says this peace "transcends all understanding."

Surrendering your anxieties to God, then, is an act of faith. Remaining joyful in suffering, peaceful in turmoil, confident in troubles does not make earthly sense, so don't try to understand this peace from an earthly point of view, from an anxious point of view. Instead, look at this peace—at this promise—from God's point of view of faith. Anchor yourself to that which you cannot see (Hebrews 11:1).

> By God's grace, we are not bound by our own ability but are empowered by Christ!
>
> "BUT HE SAID TO ME, 'MY GRACE IS SUFFICIENT FOR YOU, FOR MY POWER IS MADE PERFECT IN WEAKNESS.' THEREFORE I WILL BOAST ALL THE MORE GLADLY ABOUT MY WEAKNESSES, SO THAT CHRIST'S POWER MAY REST ON ME."
> —2 CORINTHIANS 12:9

## Hear What God *Is* Saying

You may be a Christian who does not believe you are part of "the world" in "for God so loved the world that he gave his one and only Son, that whoever believes in him shall not perish but have eternal life" (John 3:16). If so, you're allowing your anxieties to speak for God, which is never a wise thing. Allow God to speak for himself. Here are just a few of my favorite examples:

- He loves you (Deuteronomy 23:5).

- He does not want you to live in fear (Psalm 27:1).

- He knows who you are and still loves you (Psalm 139:1).

- He wants you to be with him always (John 3:16).

- Nothing can snatch you from his hand (John 10:28–29).

- His love for you will never fail (1 Corinthians 13:8).

- He says you are his precious child (1 John 3:1).

These are just a very small sample of God's promises. There are so many more! I encourage you to pick up a book that focuses just on God's promises. There are several such compilations of God's promises gleaned from Scripture.

As a baby step, memorize two or three promises that give you a sense of security and peace. Allow God's voice—instead of the voice of anxiety—to fill your heart and mind. When you listen to God's voice, Paul says God will "guard your hearts and your minds in Christ Jesus." God will guard your heart and mind. There is no stronger protection.

When you allow God to speak for himself, to speak into your life, you are in for the divine blessing of knowing God. Until now, you have spent your time and energy becoming intimately acquainted with your fears. You know when those fears happen, what they look like, and how they act. You know your fears. Doesn't God deserve at least as much of your attention?

God is "jealous for you" (2 Corinthians 11:2). I appeal to you to turn away from your anxieties and your fears. Turn, instead, to God, so you can develop a stronger and deeper relationship with him, anchoring yourself to him. Instead of spending time being attentive to your anxieties, fill your mind with thoughts of God— with his words, his promises, and his peace.

You can do this because God is on your side in this journey. Keep taking those baby steps that bring you closer and closer to peace, as you draw nearer and nearer to God. Actively do what you can do to turn away from worshiping at the altar of fear. Do all you can do and then trust God to do the rest.